THE KINDLY TRAVELLER

Retold by Susan Dickinson
Illustrated by Alison Nicholson

CARNIVAL

One day a teacher came up to Jesus and asked him how he could get to heaven. Jesus looked at the teacher and said, "You must love God with all your heart, and you must love your neighbour as much as you do yourself."

"What do you mean? Love my
neighbour? Who's that?" asked the
teacher.

"Listen, and I'll tell you a story," said
Jesus.

A man in the country of Judea was
once walking from the city of
Jerusalem to Jericho. It was a long way
and he had no friend to walk with him.
But he strode out bravely, singing as he
went to cheer himself up.

Suddenly he saw three men in front of
him, barring his way. They had been
hiding behind a rock waiting for a
lonely traveller to come along.

"Hand over your money," they said,
advancing towards him and raising
heavy wooden clubs.

Before the traveller could do anything, the men jumped on him and beat him to the ground. They tore his money from him, then kicked him over to the side of the road amongst the stones and shrubs.

Then they ran off as fast as they could.

The traveller lay there, bruised and bleeding. He was too weak to move from the side of the road.

After a while he heard the sound of another traveller approaching. Raising his head a little he saw that it was a priest coming down the road. "Help!" the man called, faintly.

The priest looked across at the man's torn clothes and bloody face. "Please God, don't let me meet the thugs who did this," he said to himself, and he hurried on without a second glance.

Some time later, another traveller approached. This one was a Levite, somebody who worked in the Temple.

The Levite noticed the man lying battered and bleeding by the rocks on the roadside and went over to look.

"Lucky it was him and not me," he thought to himself, and he pushed on quickly without stopping any longer.

A long while later, the injured man
heard the clop clop of hooves. It was a
donkey carrying a man from the
country of Samaria.

The injured man barely raised his head
to look. "There's no hope there," he
thought. "No Samaritan is going to
help me, a Jew. He might even finish
me off."

When the Samaritan saw the man and the state he was in, he immediately got off his donkey and went over to him.

"What happened?" he said. "Who did this to you?"

Without waiting for an answer, he went
to his donkey's saddle baskets and took
out oil and wine. He tore up a spare
robe he was carrying and used it to
bathe and bandage the man's wounds.

"Come with me," he said, helping the man on to his donkey's back. "We'll travel together. Don't worry, I'll take care of you."

The two of them made their way down the rocky track until they came to an inn.

At the inn, the Samaritan put his donkey in the stable and booked a room for the night. He ordered supper for the injured man and himself, then stayed with him until the following morning.

When the Samaritan left the inn he said to the innkeeper, "Keep this man here and look after him until he is strong enough to continue his journey. Here's some money. If this is not enough, when I pass here next time I'll pay you the rest."

Jesus stopped and looked at the teacher. "Which one of those three travellers was a neighbour to the man who was set upon by robbers?" he asked.

"The one who helped him and was kind to him," replied the teacher.

"You go and do the same," said Jesus.